The Water Cart

Malcolm McFarlane

The Water Cart

For Nicky, Liam and Hugh

and all people of the Paarka

The Water Cart
ISBN 978 1 76041 524 2
Copyright © Malcolm McFarlane 2018

First published 2018 by
GINNINDERRA PRESS
PO Box 3461 Port Adelaide 5015 Australia
www.ginninderrapress.com.au

Preface

It was quite a few months after my father died that I went back to his boxes of things. The packing up or tossing out of the artefacts of a life had been done as swiftly as possible following his death. What my brother and sister did not desire created a low false wall of cardboard boxes inside my garage.

After just a few days, I ceased to notice them, or at least to pay them any respect, given the family history they contained, forming as they did a convenient nudge point for the front bumper as I squeezed the car in just far enough to close the roller door behind. Then for some reason one evening, I thought this was wrong and so reversed a little, deciding to instead reacquaint myself with the contents of those boxes so hastily assembled.

Amid a heavy collection of books – varied and mostly quite old – was the worn cardboard case of a small Bible. The deep blue of the aged but intact case was faded to pale along one edge, the picture on the cover almost sepia with just a touch of colour here and there: *The Adoration of the Shepherds* – St Luke 2:16. A mother cradled her child, the focus of some attention. I discovered, however, upon lifting this fragile lid from its stiff lower portion that the volume contained therein was not a Bible.

Only just fitting into its snug surrounds, I had to lever it free with my fingers. The yellowish brown spiral-bound notebook did not look like it would contain anything from St Luke. Each page was filled with poetry: verses of a similar size, it seemed. Every leaf written on both sides and, on a dozen or so sheets of loose lined paper folded and placed inside the back cover, the same regular groupings of verse. Then resting separately beneath was a small piece of yellowed calico cloth folded roughly square, pressed almost stiff beneath the notebook. There was no title as such but at the top of the front page was written in a simple but clear flowing hand, 'Some memories and some ideas – by Jack Thomson'. Jack Thomson was my grandfather – my father's father.

I started reading his verse that afternoon, and have hardly stopped reading it since. For a few reasons, I hope you – whoever cares to read it now too – understand why I think it may be worthwhile sharing my grandfather's thoughts and experiences. My own father never mentioned any of this to me, which is something I cannot understand. Perhaps he simply never opened the box that his father had left him.

Please note that my grandfather wrote all the lines of people's speech in capital letters. I've changed that to italics just because it looked so stern if left in the original when typed. However, all the lines, spacing, spelling and lack of punctuation are as it was found.

Duncan Thomson
May 2015

Some memories and some ideas – by Jack Thomson

10 February 1967

the wheel moved for Grace
but it was no simple thing
not without torment
not without cajolery
Grace placing her slim soiled hands
upon the spokes of the timber wheel
slightly taller than she

her voice loud
in imitation of her father's
way up front
urging their horse
their almost exhausted and ageing grey mare
gerrup…caarn…gerrup I say
came the crackling deep voice from within her slight frame

the brief times of rest were welcome
but then the getting moving again
was a problem increasing with the horse's age
the horse that she'd known all her twelve years
born beside it her mother said
born between the horse and a big old mulga tree
before they could get back to town and their simple home

but the wheels were turning now
and a sweet thing it was
once moving
once underway and walking on
her father would at times let her climb up
climb up upon the cart to rest some
especially on the trips back home

the cart so much lighter once the load delivered
once the water syphoned into that tank
so they could then make for home
in good weather a week to return
their camp sites regular
perhaps a night at home with mum
then a cart filled from Darling River pools to repeat the trek once more

Grace would tell me things
and I would listen to her words and her thoughts
such a voice she had for a young girl
she would speak of all things to me
and me to her me back to her honestly
and I saw things too back in those days
I saw plenty of things a young boy maybe should not see nor hear

Grace's dad and mine both had carts
water carts that supplied the mining town of White Cliffs
except Grace's dad was not her father she let me know
but she called him dad just the same
closest to a real one I reckon I'll get
unperfect he may be
she would say while recovering from tears

they were not in business together our two fathers
nor competition either really
a separate but coordinated team I guess it was
each man would try to be at either end of the journey by the same day
so that the dry little mining camp was never too many days away
from the next cart coming in from Wilcannia
driven by either my dad or Grace's week upon week upon year

and the best thing was that on each journey
our paths would somewhere collide
Grace and I would either have a yarn and a play as the men exchanged news
or even better if it was near the end of the day
our camps would be combined
and we would help each other cook and with whatever else
happy thing that she was such a funny happy thing

that's where I remember those hands
those long slim fingers of hers
pushing at the cart wheels to get the thing on its way
carn, gerrup there
I can hear her as if it were yesterday
carn she would say
smiling cheeky and waving me on my opposite way

*

terribly dry it was
nearly all my young years out there
the Federation Drought it came to be named
but I don't recall anyone calling it such
not at the time I mean
it was just one big long dry spell
some of them camps with or without Grace were dusty old affairs

late 1890s it would have been
those camps and conversations I most recall
so much talk about Federation
exciting days they were too
looking back at least always seems so
yet at the time it was work and more of it
trying to cart some moisture within that big dry

yet the evenings were special always
just the peace and the cool
and the blanket of stars above
double special of course if with Grace
if Grace and I got to share the fire
doing all our chores but having a laugh too
and listening sometimes to the dads' conversations

clearly it was a big thing
this Federation idea
Sir Henry Parkes himself had spoken over at Broken Hill
and my dad had spoken to a bloke who was there
a fella at White Cliffs as I recall
opal miner more than likely
the place will never be the same

and that much is true
that much was true
looking back upon all these decades
it was a different world
simpler some say back in those times
but I don't know
there were complexities and things I'd rather not recall

but hope there too
and maybe that was about this Federation thing
the idea of coming together
creating something new in the world
and there were a few of us to get together
Grace and her Aboriginal mob plus Muslim cameleers
the Chinese and this mix of course of us whitefellas good and bad

a hell of a thing to try to do when you think on it
decide to gather together the separate colonies
all so very far apart back then
and connect them into something called a nation
yet despite all the protestations
all the squabbles and jealous anxieties
there was an appetite no doubt by most to come together

one evening I particularly recall
quite animated it all got too
when we camped at a point about halfway
a happy camp with Grace and her dad
until Old Tom with his bullock dray came upon us
going off about the Afghans
how they shouldn't be part of the place at all

I don't remember any part in this my father played
except him breaking Grace's dad and old Tom apart
too much rum or maybe not enough
and the curses and the pros and cons
lots of nasty stuff the details of which I don't recall
but I remember it upsetting my young head
some of the things old Tom had to say

it made no sense to me anyway
his anger at another mob
another mob who had simply arrived out there
working hard just like him
to make a living and maybe a bit more
and by crikey they were needed those cameleers
cannot imagine the place without them in those times

our horses weren't up to much really
and though Old Tom's bullock team was a mighty thing
it were awful slow
a wonderful thing to watch back in those days
the teams
colossal what they could haul
but there was no pretending they were not built for speed

the camels were a different game
a different thing entirely
and a caravan snaking its way along
across all that dust and mallee
it could shift some stuff alright
and swiftly too
at least compared to our old cart or a bullock team

perhaps it was jealousy
envy or a bit threatened Old Tom may have been
that made him launch at the cameleers as he did
a red in the face anger
spitting profanities at the fire
even after his initial rage
stinkin darky scum every one of 'em

from that night on I worried about grog and men
mostly during our turn-around nights at White Cliffs
or any night when Old Tom joined our fire
not my dad so much
he was a pretty moderate man
in all things really
but by jove I've seen some men let themselves go

Grace would go real quiet
even before I sensed there would be trouble
Grace would somehow know
start moving away a little if she could
fiddling with the wagon or go off
collecting more kindling even when it wasn't needed
just to be away from the anger and the unknown

and I would follow her of course
partly to see if she was okay
but mostly because I just liked it better
when I was with her
and even when she had that look
slightly worried and on edge I guess she was
Grace would try to turn things around from dark to light

ye followin' again so ye are Jack
remember me mum's warnin'
to us both it was
about followin' those cheeky ones
the willy-wagtails
be careful Jack that their little dancin' ways
don't lead ye off into the bush and before ye know it all lost

careful now Jack
how do ye know I ain't one
one of them cheeky willy-wagtails
dancin' and flutterin'
follow if ye like
but I don't know where I'm dancin' to
don't know where I'll fly even me

and yes what she said was true
one of Grace's mother's favourite stories
one of her favoured tales of warning to her little girl
was about those forever dancing little birds
their plump white breasts and black-hooded heads
black backs and long raised tails
with movements endless and staccato

so lively and entrancing
their energetic little dance
that young children who were careless
not thinking what they were doing
would follow without a care
and before they knew it would be lost
lost in the bush or taken by people who were surely bad

little birds of treachery it seemed
and Grace's mum had me convinced too
stay away from those tiny pretty little things
not to follow in any case
despite the attraction
to a dancing and carefree thing
the fear of becoming lost was always there

Grace was clever with her comparison
she was right to make the connection
if only at that time in fun
she was right to see herself as a dancing bird
with a path choreographed by no one
a path of mystery and possibility
a carefree yet mindful little bird

and yes I would have followed her
imagined I always would
entranced as a careless child
until she lost me
and finally just flew away
forever lost thought I of she
though I never stopped scanning the horizon

careful now Jack
I recall her coming close up to my face
a long finger pointing right up to my nose
ye must be careful what ye followin'
and why
and she turned and ran
expecting me to chase her into the half-light beyond the camp

and I did
I always would
though knowing it impossible
to catch her
I would chase
for the fun of it
and to be further from the grog and the nonsense

*

there was one week or so from back then
that shall never leave my mind
a few days now precious
from where I suspect most of my memories of her emerge
a brief time into which so many little details were packed
packed into an unexpected journey with their water cart
a few days plenty long enough together to cement a childhood bond

and all because of my father
who awoke one morning on the track feeling ill
nothing he could work out
just aching all over he kept saying
so unusual for him
a solid robust style of man
I can't recall another time he was unwell

just as he had made himself get moving
enabled the cart to continue its steady journey
determined for us to reach White Cliffs
Grace and her father we did encounter
a brief discussion and it was decided
the best thing was for me to return with them
better I get back to Wilcannia than stay with a dad who was poorly

I remember too protesting meekly
suggesting wouldn't it be better for me to stay
to look after him if he was crook for a time
yet as I recall with most things
once his mind was set
there was precious little chance of swaying it
be a good boy son said the moderate man with a firm shake of my hand

I didn't know
I had no sense at all
that it would be the last time I saw him
my father
an earnest and hard-working man
and I think also he knew nothing of what was to consume him
so casual was our final farewell

it was the first time we had been apart
certainly the only time I recall a whole night without him
yet with Grace and her dad
quickly became the logical place for me to be
we just presumed my father would be ok
I would instead help them
and wait for dad at home in Wilcannia

I would be a good boy
as my father requested
but to be honest I was never much of a renegade
calm compared to most when I look back upon my time
even back then as a child
perhaps I guess because of him
I've just kept on at it despite what life threw my way

and so my clearest and fondest
memories of Grace
are special too
mixed as they are with the loss of my father
those few days of innocent closeness with her
imbued with the shock the aching pain
some days later upon hearing of his sudden death

I remember a large gruff-looking man
coming over to Grace and I
pretty much as soon as we got back to town
her father was with this man unknown to me
also looking grim
having exchanged a few words slightly beyond our hearing
they both walked over quietly and the serious man began to speak

I hear you are Duncan Thomson's son
he asked in a voice trying to be soft
despite his lofty frame and dark drooping moustache
funny the things you remember
I never did see him again
nor do I know who he was
significant enough a man though in that river town to carry
heavy news to a boy

I am very sorry to tell you son
that your father passed on three nights back
a good decent hard working man
you need to know that's how all here thought of him
died of some form of malady unknown
and so he was to be buried just this morning in White Cliffs
may the Lord rest his honest soul

and then I remember Grace
staring at me before crying
with me sobbing too
and her hugging
holding me tight
like she would never let me go
and me not wanting her to ever let me go

so swift the decline
my father one day as strong as ten men
then so suddenly in the ground
so swift also that day
my spirits high at having spent such a time with Grace
then plummeting with no warning at all
my world was turned completely upside down

and what a few days they had been
with Grace and her father
strange how the same path travelled so many times
could with a different companion
become a road as if previously unknown
the same dry creek beds and stony plains
with her were new playgrounds to explore

my willy-wagtail was on her own country
flitting about it
at times on the ground
and then without warning briefly in the air
she tried to be a good girl
or so it seemed
for her dad she did try to be good though often failed

harsh words would come from the cart if ever she did wander
her father's sudden deep and urgent cry
a mixture of anger and concern rocketing across the dry ochre plains
Grace
where are you now child
Grace
to which the girl shook from her wanderings and dutifully returned

how many times I got to tell ye girl
don't be wandering
don't matter how often we've followed this 'ere track
once ye start to wander away well
every mulga and mallee look the same
ye be swallowed up out there my little girl
beyond the reach of my bellowing ye'd be gone in this heat soon enough

he would grab her by the shoulders
bending down to look into her brown eyes
that tried to evade him with tears and shame
he would squeeze her shoulders and shake her slightly
not to hurt her but in frustration
full of anxiety for the girl
and fear that the precious thing would be lost to him

and each time she transgressed
each time she wandered or did some other thing to anger the man
the harsh reprimand would conclude with him holding her tight
he would hold her in silence until the sobbing abated
and as much as she feared him
could predict neither his temper nor mood
she sensed he cared and that he was her true protector

come child
he said as she wiped her face and was swung up onto the wagon
rest a bit up there
we have a way to go yet today
and this old horse here needs to keep moving
she's strugglin' enough through this sandy stretch
even with the tank empty and heading for home

after such times
I'd trail a little behind
her father would pace out ahead
ahead of the slow plod of their horse
stepping out his frustrations and upset
and Grace would stay sitting up on the wagon high
quiet and looking sad

it made sense for me to stay back a way
still there with them but sensing some space was required
Grace would maintain her silence
eyes looking straight out ahead
towards her stepping father but perhaps way past him too
from behind I would watch her head of roughly cropped dark hair
almost still as her body shifted with the many movements of the cart

and after some time
and it could be quite a long time
her father would stop and turn back towards her
at which the horse would pull up without instruction
and Grace would be asked if she wanted to stay up there
her reply would be a simple *no*
and my friend would return to my side

on one such day she even briefly held my hand
funny the things you remember
she must have been feeling particularly fragile
and there was I
her friend
walking beside
neither judging nor scolding her

she wanted to show me things along the track
as I wished to show her things too
different little spots we'd noticed over our many separate journeys
as if even though we had nothing material to share
we could at least offer up these small secrets
these personal things
to someone we trusted and who maybe cared

a campsite by a soft dry creek bed
was special to both of us
if though for different reasons
Grace found a tiny little dark brown gecko
fussing over it as she revealed it to the sun
its loose bark shelter lifted away
the little thing fitting easily into the palm of her sheltering hand

the place was special to me also
simply because it was dad's favourite camp site
he'd say so every time we pulled up there
and a few times even when the day was far from done
when we could have pressed on further easily
he'd decide to stop early for a change
unable to go past his favourite spot

favourite he said
not just because of the beauty of the place
the simple spare elegance of the shady trees
and the soft orange-pink earth all around
it was special for him I think because he was twice stuck there alone
marooned for days on end by sudden rain
and the rapid rise in a creek bed otherwise dry

it took Grace to discover a little gecko though
a tiny silent thing
a scared wee living thing
amid all that vast open country
its skin almost a velvet
only Grace could reveal such a thing
and share the beauty of the small creature with her friend

I remember Grace holding me
coming back again and again
to give me comfort without words
that evening
the awful day
that I heard my father had died
so kind she was in her sadness

such a long time ago now
hard to recall the exact sequence of events
but within those following few days
my dad dead though such a young strong man
and with him my whole life compass disappeared
those first few days of shock and tears
I gratefully stayed with Grace and her family

it was decided that I should at least see the grave
and so I went with Grace and her dad
leaving after a day or two
on their regular journey
that was so irregular to me
without my father now
knowing that no other cart would be coming the other way

Grace did her best to try to cheer me
but some of her lightness had gone
and any time I did laugh at her
for some funny thing she did or said
I felt guilty for it
sad as I was to the core
sad that dad could laugh no more

yet Grace would not allow despair
she would not let the gloomy clouds stay for long
she would look for some light
create some kind of spark
to distract or to cheer
lead the way to a happier place
and try to keep me there

especially in those first few days
when I returned to White Cliffs with them
the path the same yet so very different without him
not like those few days I'd spent with Grace before
when I thought dad would be there again
so carefree it all seemed before
and how serious and foreign it all was thereafter

hot it was too
not that heat was ever far away
out on that track
but that trip seemed especially so
even the nights warm
and that's when heat is really felt
when the cool relief of night never comes

dust of course
a part of everything
not a full dust storm on that trip but awful dry
when with just the slightest bit more than a breeze
you'd be protecting eyes from it again
yet the nights were so often calm
a stillness to amplify the few sounds that were out there

I remember lying there on a night without a moon
an almost perfect quiet it was
stars above so thick and close
and so calm I could hear the steady breath
of my friend not far from me
curled up as she always slept curled tight
sharing the soft dry earth between the old wagon and an ember fire

we would have talked until her father told us to sleep
then whispers for a while
before sleep caught up
before Grace slipped from whispers
into the steady breath of dreams
the crackle of a slow fire the only music there
a wild dog howl sometimes far but sometimes near

each day on that journey to my father's grave
I awoke in the hope of another wagon coming the other way
perhaps it took me each step
each expectant step along that familiar route
to realise that all would never be the same
I would not walk with my father again
nor would a happy friend be coming towards me somehow somewhere

there was not even a sign on that trip
of some of the characters we would often see
a team of cameleers in their long proud line
or Old Tom and his stolid bullock team
we instead stepped out a particularly silent journey
or so I remember it to be
appropriate I suppose for a boy approaching a new grave

I do remember
staring down at freshly piled earth
a child's moist eyes upon his father's grave
wanting to forever gaze upon him
yet also compelled to look away
noticing the proper headstones all around while my father yet had none
and how many children within that sad fence there did lay

the heat of early summer
was there on that difficult day
a faint wispy afternoon breeze
the smell of turned earth
the still settling earth
and the slim hand of Grace
after a moment grasping mine

*

that evening it was
or perhaps we spent another day before the turn-around
there was much discussion about my father's cart
the pub gathering became something of a wake
Grace's father had gone there to check over the cart
and our horse still stabled there
our beautiful black gelding in the backyard of that drinking hole

the strong but gentle beast seemed to smooch around us
Grace and I
as we waited for the conversations inside
sometimes loud
and the drinking
to finally cease
waiting for men to spill out from the last shafts of kerosene light

awful smart I'm thinkin'
most horses
and this one especially
Grace commented as we waited
look at him following you around eh
wants to be close as he can
and wants close to ye dad too I'm thinkin'

I did love that horse
Parkes my father called him
no name he had for the first year or so we had him
at least that's how I recall
but then there was all the talk after Sir Henry's visit
the many conversations about Federation
though not all agreed with him he was admired that was so

then once the news was about of the great man's demise
a good solid horse
a good solid name
leading us on dead or alive
dad would say with a wry smile
to anyone who commented
to anyone wanting to challenge a horse's name

come 'ere then Parkes me boy
Grace's father declared as he emerged
louder than when he had entered
some hours before
louder and embracing the gentle strong horse
louder and emotional and breathing rum
we'll be ye family now

surprised though I was at this news
the decision did make sense
and was a good thing for all
and they were family
those work horses on the track
part of our lives
essential for our lives back then

amid cups of rum and whatever else
a few things had been determined
the ageing horse belonging to Grace's father
would be remaining at the White Cliffs Hotel
replaced quite logically by the strong and calm Parkes
our cart however was another thing indeed
attracting as it had the attention of the local constabulary

Grace was distraught at first with this news
made no better by her father's
enthusiasm in his jovial telling
anxious that she would never again see her Bow
the horse she had been born beside
don't be silly child her father chided
she'll be 'ere for many a year running simple errands around

his play on words created laughter only for him
she'll have the perfect however many latter years
helpin' out here with her bowed back will old Bow
thus making Grace cry all the more
and she ran off directly into the dark
and as I hoped and imagined
to the care of the poor horse she loved

I remember too
the firm grip
like an iron grip it was
of her father's hand as I began to run off after her
let her be lad
she'll just be going across the way
to cry with that old broken backed mare that is ours

then followed
for a fair length of time as I recall
an outline of my future
my future according to Grace's father
both short and long term
some of it reasoned and some with the vapours of alcohol articulated
and of it all this much my memory retains

we'll be set to travel not tomorrow but the next day
and return to Wilcannia with Parkes in the lead we shall
we'd best forget about your cart for the time being though me boy
I'm not sure what it is
but there are things about it that has some questions raised
I know not enough to say any more
yet there are German traders in opals and Chinese too hovering around

and so it was that I heard of the rumours surrounding my father
you'll come back with young Grace and me
on our cart but now with your dad's horse out front
whereupon at Wilcannia I'm thinking of a meeting of sorts
with a man from a property upstream
as I've just now heard a good place
always keen for a good lad to lend a hand

I remember thanking him
yet thinking too
either right then or perhaps a bit later on
when I was slightly less numb with my grief
that this man was suddenly deciding my fate
he took our horse and would then wave me goodbye
but I was just a sad and lonely child

my question about the cart I do recall though
why can't we take both your cart and mine
said me a boy of twelve
alone in the dark at the back of a pub closed
wedged between the warm neck of the horse I loved
and the stooped and swaying bearded face
of an unpredictable man

both carts and horses
questioned he
as he turned and gazed up at the darkness and the stars
the close ceiling of stars in that inland desert sky
not likely lad no
you'll not have me drivin' two carts and horses
not to mention Grace and you on that track no

and besides
as I said before
your father's cart must stay here
in the compound so it is and will stay
but enough of that now
it is what it is
as I said is how it shall be

though I would have been happier to sleep that night with Parkes
I was made to follow him back to their camp
where we discovered Grace up on the cart
curled up and in tears
scolding her father for taking so long
and explaining that she'd had a visit that had made her scared
at which once she calmed some she was pressed for more

Grace mentioned of a group of Chinese
triggering a cascade of threats and curses from the man she called a father
and so before she could explain anything further she fairly screamed
stop and listen for a moment will ye
they didn't touch me or so much as raise a voice
which quelled some the imperfect man
but they kept asking the same thing over and again

her father quietened and listened some more
what then child
what did they want of you or of perhaps me
to which all my friend could reply
I think something about Jack's dad
that they wanted to see his cart
he had something for them

the man who Grace called her father
thought long over the girl's explanation
then as he motioned us to bed down beneath the wagon calmly said
think no more on them child
they shan't bother you no more
sleep safe tonight
and tomorrow we'll be on the track with a strong horse in the lead

*

it struck me as interesting then
and more so as time went on
that Old Tom appeared that very next morning
unusually early I awoke to the sounds of preparation
of Grace rising near me
her sleep-crumpled face looking quizzically at mine
then the rasping high voice of Old Tom to her father

all I am sayin' is you are wise to be gettin' away
not one of 'em I'd be trustin' me
Old Tom had also been at the pub the night before
and whether it was following from conversations there
or that word of Grace's visit the night before had already spread
I was not to know
nor did I straight away enquire of the obviously brooding man her father

unusual though I remember thinking
that following a night of drinking
he was up with such energy and intent so early
something was unsettling him
and it in some way involved my father
yet I chose not to press for information
not only through fear of the man

for a grieving young boy
there was suddenly amid the sadness and loss
another layer of complexity
that the dearly departed had been imperfect
or even worse involved in something quite wrong
dark thoughts also came to me in those next strange days
that it was not from *a malady unknown* from which my dad had died

of that journey back to Wilcannia
I of course recall Grace and her kind friendship
and one brief conversation with her father
only a day or so along the track
I missing my own father all the more
at the sight of things he enjoyed along the way
bright red tails of black cockatoos or the circling arc of a solitary kite

Grace's dad had been praising Parkes
the horse I would always consider my own
the horse I loved because of his steady calm
its new driver was full of praise for his obedience and power
by the lord I wish I'd had me one like him years before
it's a wonder lad that ye father didn't get along this track in half the time
sure Parkes could do it if ye pushed 'im

my face must have betrayed anxieties
for without me saying a word came a reply
don't worry none son
I shan't be doin' that to old Parkes here
I won't flog 'im none
think too much of your father for that
he's a fine workhorse just the same

it worried me though
he was not a bad man
simply good at times
the ways he cared for Grace mostly
yet there was an inconsistency or something about him
and grateful as I was for his help there was an opportunism let me say
he was certainly not a scratch on the man I believed my father to have been

was my father murdered do you think
I heard myself ask that imperfect man
words perhaps surprising me as much as he
the thought was occupying my mind
yet I did not expect anything to part my lips just at that time
such an idea came the reply dismissively
your father was a true and good soul to all

I doubt that I expected any more of an answer than I received
my intent perhaps designed as an indication that I did have a brain
and eyes and ears my head also contained
my heart was truly broke
for many a long time
but some answers I would one day find
that twelve year old quietly determined

*

whether by design or chance
on that final trip we again made camp
at my father's favourite site
the same place where Grace had shared
her treasured dark velvet gecko hiding under bark
and that much was happily the same
beneath the same leopard-wood tree she soon found that little friend

her father scowled as if we were idlers
so we assured him there was plenty of kindling to collect
which was true enough
the first task of mine too
on many a journey with my father
to gather up a good few armfuls
for the evening rituals

and though I have made many a camp
many a happy fire over what is now a long life already
there's nothing in my experience to match the burn you get
the intense slow burn of the coals
from those timbers of the western plains
such hard slow growing tough old tortured trees
a mulga limb is like lifting a lump of steel

my infrequent visits out that way
over the last few decades now gone
were not the same if a fire at night was not built
and built right with mulga or mallee
it would easily reach until dawn
a sweet enough sight to awake to and rekindle
that the camp might remain another day another night

and the smells
the clean dry earthy smoke
from those particular fires
even in the cooling ashes
a comforting odour would envelop all
as if the embrace of nature and so many years before
the camp fires of centuries and those shared with my only father

of all the fires though
the coals beside that small dry creek bed meant most to me
Grace sensed my quiet mood
and left me well alone
though she was right there by my side
she left me with my thoughts of my dad
close as he was in that one place especially so

even her father
her infrequently sensitive father
either through ignorance or perception
allowed me unusually to roam a little that afternoon
enabled me to walk up and down that empty rivulet
at times with Grace and then without her
yet always with the quiet memory of my father suddenly gone

watercourses such as that small one in that part of the inland
were usually dry
empty serpentine vessels
until a storm or hopefully lengthy rain
would transform the flat-bedded trench
into a broiling ochre wonder
gathering moisture briefly before disgorging it again onto the grateful plains

that afternoon though
and for too many afternoons before
there was not a hint of rain
the earth was parched truly parched
the soft sandy burnt-orange soil upon which I walked alone
at times spilling up over the top of my ankle boots
the leather boots my father had not long before been so proud to afford

it had been dry so long
I could barely remember that watercourse or others
in any way moist let alone in full flow
the torrent only ever temporary
but with a legacy of damp
holding still pools for a time
cradling green and all manner of life unexpected

just as Grace caught up to me
checking on me
putting her hand on my shoulder
I began to realise that even since that last visit there
that last camp with my father
not so very long at all before
this place had already changed

what is it then Jack
what's troubling you of a sudden
I can still hear that deep quiet voice
her words always so clear
spoken as honest as the hot pale blue sky we stood below
ye know ye dad would be happy we were here
don't be troubled so

it was of course true
Grace knew my thoughts were never so very far from him
yet at that particular time
I was standing looking down and around
not as some forlorn orphan child
but as a boy trying to understand
the scars in the land before him

pigs been through here look
I remember almost spitting out the words
dad hated them so
hated what he'd seen them do to land
them wild ones gettin' around so much now
every time we spotted some or where they'd been
he'd get as cranky as I've seen him be

we walked on through the worst of it
yard upon yard of roughed-up rooted-up dry ground
a huge stretch of bank dug away
and up around the acacias and the saltbush plain
it just didn't seem right
like some beastly machine
had churned through without feeling or care

then we talked some
about how of all places
that one creek special to us both
and to my dad
had been trashed by rotten pigs
and I recall Grace making mention
of her mother and the land

it ain't just pigs ye know though
and if ye were to listen to my mum
sheep and cattle and horses too
camels even now
are all to blame
and all things brought here a course
by you whitefellas eh

in my memory's eye
Grace would always deliver profundities with a smile
as she did that day
not making a joke out of the sad reality
but her directness and her smile
and how at the same time she pushed me away with a giggle
another challenge to chase that cheeky pee-wee bird

ignorance is part of history I suppose
part of the history of everywhere
and so looking back now
upon all the things done to this land
it's easy I guess to excuse a lot of what them earlier settlers done
but I don't know about it all from simply being naive
even me as a boy all those years ago could see what was good and what bad

*

the return to Wilcannia
became another passage of days still dear to me now
it was when I felt nearest to Grace
with our closeness only leading to an almost final separation
two nights maybe three with she and her family
before pathways were decided for us both
pushed along quite opposing roads

it was the most time I had spent with her mother too
a Paarkintji woman hooked up somehow
with this man Grace called her father
a quiet careful woman of almost ebony black skin
her slight frame not much beyond that of her girl's
dwarfed totally by the man of the house
a bearded thick-set yet stooped white man

I recall arriving at their house
a simple structure down along the Menindee Road
not unlike my own on the north side of town
though in truth without mother there
ours lacked the sense that it was home
my father and I both
more comfort perhaps under canvas or stars along the track

like many a place out there in those days
Grace's was a plain enough affair
dirt floor
a main room with the fireplace and table as you stepped in
and another space off behind for sleeping
their front little veranda had a bushy sort of sapling wall end too
with a stretcher bed that was my camp while with them there

in truth I cannot recall if it was that first night or not
but the conversations involving me
and those overheard
appear now as if spoken only yesterday
beginning with the return of Grace's dad
walking back from town
where he was to meet a man about an opportunity for a young boy

ye have to be thinkin' on ye prospects lad
and there's more for ye perhaps than walkin' this track each week
thing is
I know a man who's down from Kallara Station
big block just upstream you may know
he be willing to let ye ride up with him
and if ye hook in and have a go well it might just be the spot for ye

I don't remember making any kind of reply
though I dare say I thanked him and such
but what I do recall is just feeling sad
kind of heavy and sunken down with the news
and I remember the face of Grace
quiet and looking down
as if a mirror to my mood entirely

more was suggested that evening too
about my prospects on such a big property
a million acres or so he said it to be
as places out that way were then
likely with some schooling too
opportunities unending
yet all involved leaving the only friend I knew

your pee-wee bird is going for a walk
come with me Jack
there's music off in town somewhere
I had been lying awake on my stretcher
a head full of too many things
wondering if they were all sleeping inside
before Grace's face emerged before mine

she assured me that once off snoring
her father would not wake till dawn
and your mother I remember worrying
to which Grace smiled and replied
I told her what I'm about
and she's ok
and she knows there's no comin' between music and me

and so we were gone
skipping and running and giggling
all the way along into town
following in the dark the slim shadow of a road
and the faint trail of music somewhere
bare wisps of sound that were at times clear
coming and going on the breeze

we headed to each pub we knew
but every one sat dark and quiet so late it was in the night
and just as we were about to head for the river
thinking it must be a gathering down there somehow
near the fine Court House buildings
the music became louder and suddenly close
laughter and a violin clear helped us find our way

in a small but neat solid looking house
of that fine blonde Wilcannia sandstone
in the centre of a large block with rose gardens
thorns soon found in the dark by me
through solid window panes of glass
a luxury found in neither Grace's hut nor my own
there came waves of melody of laughter of happiness of a home

we could not help but be cheered
peering from behind a nest of roses quite tall
their perfume I smell still
almost honey thick so it seemed
on that perfect stolen night
of music and forgetting
of friendship and honesty

though no musician myself at any time
my love I think for it
my sense of wonder at what music can bring
was without doubt born that night
watching grown women and men in their finery
occasionally become part of the window frame
a swirl of dancing and beauty and smiles

no sense waiting for an invitation
announced Grace
grabbing my arm
thrusting us into the open dark dirt spaces
of the garden dance floor
a rough kind of waltz it was too
me not protesting but knowing nothing of what my feet were for

and what's the worst that can happen then
teased Grace as I worried aloud
of being found in some unknown person's yard
and so we scuffed up that dirt floor undiscovered
two souls who for a brief time had not a care in the world
danced on until breathless us both
and a dog roused nearby to urge us on

though even as we scurried away
down the long loamy bank of the river almost dry
that music seemed still to cascade behind us
and perhaps of such quality that we heard none complain
who it was playing that night I would never know
but in those times before such things as radio and recorded sound
the chance for music was a living and a golden thing

oh Jack what I wouldn't give to be able to dance
I mean move proper and can you imagine knowing how to play
a piano or one of them fiddles back there
even in the darkness of the night
I'm sure I could sense clearly Grace's smile and inner glow
music for her clearly was beyond joy
it was a wonder she longed to immerse herself in

the music did finally cease
or maybe we again went beyond its reach
dissolved back into the rest of the world
of silence or at least only of sounds more mundane
the world more ordinary without musicians
or so it suddenly seemed to me
magic twirls and imagining replaced by reality and the tactile

we determined not to walk straight back down the same track
but along the river some before cutting up to their home
there were still a few hours of darkness surely
and though unspoken we did want to spend whatever time as one
happy to amble along
sharing thoughts and dreams
and all in between

Grace said that we could turn up at The Bend
which amused me as that was how that whole river was laid
bend upon bend of the Darling
or Paarka as Grace called it to me
bend sweeping back upon bend
and at the time during that awful long dry spell
there was barely a linking of stagnant pools

The Bend was some way down
and special as it was her mother's favourite spot
me mum likes to go there all the time
always good for a fish
and close to our home
a funny thing
but she is so much happier when she's down there

we had walked down the long soft angled bank
the bank a deep crusty loam in the dry
to sit up along a dead heavy limb of one of the many Redgums collapsed
surrendered its foothold on the ancient soil some years before
the hard trunk and thick limbs pointing down into a muddy pool
instead of stretching up grand into an endless expanse of sky
hastened thus perhaps by paddle-wheels and other new practices of man

and though we had known each other it seemed all our years
neither of us could recall a time when together we were down there
at the Wilcannia end of the endless track
not uncommon for a camp to be shared along the way
or delays meaning we were in White Cliffs briefly the same
her father and mine
exchanging news of the conditions ahead and who or what seen

it shouldn't matter where we hooked up
but things had now changed
my father was dead
and her's seemed intent on seeing me get up and away
we sat straddling the age and water-smoothed limbs
facing each other and quiet for a time
our young legs barely able to stretch around the girth of the timber long fallen

did your mum have a favourite place that you know
maybe somewhere ye dad might have mentioned
the question surprised me more than some
I had not before spoken to Grace of her
well I somehow from somewhere replied
there's a question alright
my only memory of my mother is a small photo that's up on that impounded cart

do you know then how she died my friend carried forth
with her typical interest and care
and happy to reflect upon mostly unknowns
well my father has said it was disease
the cholera he would respond when asked
and then though another time he mentioned she was with child
and complications that did unfold

the response of my friend
simple silence
no more questions required
nor obvious comments about loss
something we both had been schooled in
and so my thoughts turned to her
a question I had for her

and so your father Grace
what memories do you have of he
and as if the question was expected
after a quiet moment came her honest reply
never did know him no
and long dead too
at least as my mother tells it

a cameleer
and don't you look all surprised
even in this nearly nothin' dark
I can see through your eyes Jack Thomson ye know
yep I got Afghan in me seems true
just like white fellas and them Chinese
been with women scared just like my mum

we must have walked quite some more
before either felt the need to speak again
I remember being sensibly quiet
as we passed by a solitary paddle steamer
hopelessly marooned but perhaps still home to an idle crew
it too had lost its bet with the dry
a final remaining pool shrunk to mud beneath its shallow hull

Grace had said that the quickest way
back up from the river to her home
was through the main cemetery
a notion I thought nothing more than a tease
until we were quite suddenly walking among the graves
up over this way she motioned and grasped my hand
reassurance at least that we were both afraid

a cemetery usually
a place for respectful silence
yet our conversation reignited through there
some comfort in hearing our voices
above the sound of a roo being surprised and bounding away
or the thump of other creatures lurking
whether real or in darkness imagined

a shame that your father is so far from you
said Grace
giving voice to my thoughts at that very same time
but he'll be up there yet look
up in them stars don't you see
as she waved a fluid limb above her head
though still marching on to be free of those eerie surrounds

following her as I was
with thoughts of my father
and a mother unknown
grasping her hand yet
as she walked faster than me just as ever
I paid no heed
to the direction our path was taking

at best I was possibly conscious
of the large trees of the river
the monumental river redgums
gradually thinning out to just a solitary specimen here and there
as we ventured further from the watercourse itself
and beyond the immediate flood zone
the path then cutting through mallee with saltbush enclosing

maybe he's buried in here somewhere
Grace suggested of her unknown father
an idea to which I of course agreed
still upset with myself for losing my bearings
you must set your own compass son
and be true to it
dad's calm reprimand when I'd failed to get a direction right with him on the cart

so he died in Wilcannia then your father
I asked with our hearts pounding not so hard
as we rejoined the Menindee Road now near to her home
I don't know if the whole truth be told
but I think it to be so
how exactly though
seems about as clear as that death of your dad

we slowed as the house became close
Grace wanting neither for our absence to be revealed
nor what she had to say overheard
thing is Jack
whether it the rum talking earlier tonight or not I ain't sure
but my father that you know he said to my mum
he feared your father was slain by the same hand as killed my dad

we of course had to say our goodnights
get into our separate stretchers before being revealed
but in a delirium of confused affection
I remember holding Grace close for a moment in the dark
and she holding me and with a whisper to my ear
thanks for the dance Jack
and let's never us forget that music eh

*

in a good season
with the river full
I could have travelled by boat to Kallara
the steamers went up there to Tilpa and then just as far again
all the way to Bourke for the wool
but water was not an option that year
when I was to head off on that new life of mine

Grace's father had a spot for me on a wagon
heading off that next day
I remember him bringing out a mug of tea
waking me with his plans for the day
the day already warm
us both having slept late
for very different reasons

Grace
he called louder than he needed
as if she was far off into the scrub
on one of her meanders out along the track
leaving him anxious and wondering
ye'd best come and say farewell to Jack
late already and he has to start a stockman's life

a sleepy Grace emerged
with her mother she came up to me
and we shook hands
my friend said nothing before heading back inside
but her mother with a clear tear in her eyes
handed me a slim bedroll and some bread
hope to see you again eh good boy

and so we walked
away from the small house their home
back into the centre of town
and though I knew it stupid to ask
and what the answer may be
I ventured just the same
so there wouldn't be work and some school for Grace too

her father turned back to me
striding out ahead as he was
she'll be with me on the cart for a few trips yet
his voice indicating no debate would be had
and before long she'll be going to duties somewhere
one of the homesteads heading south is me hope
but no schooling no not for her

and the man who Grace called her father
had a way of speaking that made something final
the last word on something
at least when he spoke to a boy of twelve
he may have sensed the disappointment in me
seen my shoulders drop
but that was the end of it regarding education and his woman's girl

the horse and cart of my expectations
turned out to be a large wagon and team
camels contracted in harness and resting on haunches
ten I remember counting in awe
five pairs sitting in meditation
long eyelashes looking down long faces held high and calm
as if announcing that no horizon would be too far

I had of course seen many camels before
the town was thriving with them
paddle steamers were a wonder too but only when the river was high
the port of Wilcannia was a hub but often like that year left dry
the camel had become a better option than horse or bullock dray
we had crossed paths on the track many a time
watched them steadily approach from behind to overtake our water dray

then there was the fury of the likes of Old Tom
bullockies who saw them as a threat very real
blaming the Afghans and their turbaned heads
their frugality and non-drinking ways
with all that was wrong with his own circumstance
rather than seeing it for what it was
a team of camels were superior out there to any bullock team

sad as I was about leaving Grace my friend
I also recall that young boy me
being fairly swept up in the excitement of it all
a dozen or so men busy with the wagon
tying the last of the huge pile down
boxes and tea chests and all manner of tools and supplies
plus another young man checking paperwork with a clerk from the store

that store itself was quite an enterprise
and it then had the urgency of a business still new
not so many months before
my father had proudly marched me in for my new leather boots
Knox and Downs where you can purchase everything
at least that was what they claimed
and one look at that bulging wagon was something of an affirmation

swing yeself up there boy
said Mr Mac the young man with a bundle of papers in hand
I had watched Grace's father motion me to wait at the wagon
then step over to speak briefly to this fellow in charge
who soon came across to shake my hand
tapping on a small space at the rear of the wagon's backboards
squeeze yeself in there or else do as a native and walk

for his part Grace's father said little
as was his way when not with grog
but he urged me to get up as suggested
you'll have plenty of chances to use them young legs
rest when ye can may be lesson number one for thee
and then he stayed with me all the while
the hour or so until departure I remember thinking it kind that he stayed

all I knew was that we would take the Tilpa Road
on the river's western side
the road followed the Darling to Bourke
our destination Kallara Station perhaps halfway along
some distance just beyond Tilpa
all these places I had never been
as I sat travelling backwards knowing nothing of the time to journey's end

young Mr Mac did of course have a full surname
though I cannot recall after all these years
what followed his particular Mac is now lost to me
it was no doubt mentioned but Mr Mac was what he preferred
and right from that first day
I saw him as a significant man
young but with thoughtfulness and intent

he rode a tall chestnut mare
swift and up and down and around the team
assessing all as we got fully underway
even before we left the last of the buildings of the town
he came behind to check on me once more
alright there then young Jack
you seem to have your gaze fixed upon something

he was right too
and his perception quite amazed me
of all the things his mind could be occupied with then
he noticed what was going on with me
just looking over at the old house sir
me dad and I lived over the way
that was all there to me

he said nothing in reply just then
but before long appeared back behind again
riding all right up there then
coo-ee if you spot something amiss
and sorry too lad
to hear of your father's passing
my uncle mentioned that he was quite a man

the uncle to whom Mr Mac referred
was the manager of Kallara Station
and the reason as it turned out
for me having a space on that rig
it was no small thing
Grace's father had done for me
connecting up with such a place at that time

even during those first few hours
I had a sense that I was going to something substantial
the very make-up of the travelling party
spoke volumes about the whole enterprise
two men up front on the wagon
another on horseback plus Mr Mac
not to mention the trio of cameleers constantly attending their beasts

and when we pulled up for a break
or made camp for the night
all that too seemed somehow organised
each person going about their tasks steadily
and being pretty gentle with me I have to say
no more questions about my father
though I had the sense that my circumstances were known

not that it was strange at all back then
to have a boy my age as an extra hand
no such thing as regular school beyond the town
learning came from everywhere
and good fortune it was indeed
to find yourself in decent company
with people who'd take the time to teach a young fella such as me

on that first camp
we snuck in amongst some mighty river gums
the sparse ground beneath their shade
and a campsite fire clearly used before
a regular stopping place it seemed
for ours and other teams
though not far east from the route I'd often taken but all new ground to me there

as I would have done once stopped with dad
I struck out to look for firewood
an easy task in most parts there
just the same it was quietly appreciated
I went about it of course with energy
as rightly taught to do
to which Mr Mac made some nice remark for the whole party to hear

I noticed too that the cameleers
took their team unhitched a little away
and there they stayed by a separate fire
which puzzled me once I realised
my query to Mr Mac as to why
seemed to both intrigue him and delight the others in our circle
that's just how they like it to be and so might I add do we

life revolved around a fire in those times
whether in the simple quarters I came to share
the main homestead too
or the station's busy kitchen
all involved a fire
which of course needed to be made then tended
and often providing more than just obvious warmth

a fire a new born babe and the sea
Mr Mac often proclaimed
when joining a camp fire circle
or perhaps when there was a break in conversation
the three things in this world
that provide endless fascination
what do you say

I learned over time that these words
said so often by the same man
required no response from anyone listening
yet on that first night for me with that company
a day's trek north of Wilcannia
on the way to a future unknown to me
I found some courage in the silence to reply

no doubt that is true sir
for a fire such as this
and any baby I have seen
yet I must confess
that as of yet sir
I am yet
to experience the sea

his response was lengthy and heartfelt
and I recall too the reaction of the others to my words
of the three other men present with us
decent fellows all and a spread of ages between
Samuel very young and Theo of middle age
it was only Henry by then quite old
who confirmed that he had been to the sea

Mr Mac at this saw an invitation
to speak at length
and in his fine way of talking
to regale us of his journeying
and in particular the passage from his native Scotland
tens years or so prior
a youth he said *not much more beyond the age of young Jack here*

it is a mighty thing most surely
and vast beyond your wildest imaginings
can be the calmest and most relaxing of places
or a hell of fury amid one of many uncertain storms
and the effect it can have upon the senses
the salt smell pungent and the breeze and the spray
constant change and nature's wonder just like this fire here I say

and yet
and yet
the young man of enthusiasm continued his tale
there are parallels I see out upon this land
for it is a similar feeling I have on some days
when rising from camp on many a clear morning here
you need only crest the slightest cairn to sense the whole curve of this sphere

laying my head down that evening
on the slim bedroll thanks to the kindness of Grace's mother
staring up at stars unending
again on soft soil but beside a wagon so different to before
and my cheeky pee-wee bird far too far away
I cried that night I remember
hoping more than anything that my sobs would go unheard

what choked me I suppose
was the speed
the swiftness bad and good
of what had come my way
the intensity of feelings upon me
of love and loss and possible betrayal
inequities in the roll of life's dice

*

so when then Henry
I asked on the next day's journey
were you at sea
the one campfire of the night before
and the openness of all
had so quickly let even me a young boy
start to feel a part of their team

not at sea as such lad
but been there plenty of times
no I was on the paddle steamers only
that's how I come to be here
up and down this stretch many a time
down to Wentworth ye know
and on occasion all the way to the mouth I'd go

another man who'd lived a life of adventure
thoughts that must have formed something like my reply
for I remember him clearly saying that as good a life as it was
it was nothing compared to what he now had
finally he felt not constantly on the move
you have a chance to be still out here
and there are no better bosses than Mr Mac and the owners too

I pressed him for details of life on the steamers
my only experience that of a boy from the bank in Wilcannia
watching them load or unload when the river high
thinking how grand it must have been
to steam off downstream
new country around every bend
Henry smiled at my enthusiasm that must have seemed to have no end

steady up there boy
though what you say be not untrue
there was plenty of work in it besides
hard yards too many a time
coaxing those old girls across sandbars and snags
not to mention the constant scrambling
along these banks to find enough timber for boilers so hungry

and then of course there are times such as these
the Murray not quite as bad
but this Darling River here is more often than not just as she lies now
a series of ponds with no show of work for a steamer crew
give me no talk ever boy of jumping a steamer eh
when one does finally again ply its way up to here
railway too no doubt soon so a steamboat future is unsure

by the time we approached Kallara Station
Sam and Theo were also better known to me
both quiet enough fellows sharing duties at the reins
the older Theo seeming to have the task on that journey
to teach the young Sam something of working with camels
and a large wagon heavy with essential supplies
he needs just to remember it's not his flash new colt he's astride

voices raised between the two I came to expect within a day
yet around each campfire
they were again as amicable as two men could be
both taking their work seriously
and so the teaching of new skills could lead to emotions raised
yet my presumption that evening they were father and son
met with what could be at best described as mixed reactions

Henry and Mr Mac I thought would die from their laughing
in tears they both soon were
while Sam and Theo could only glare at me
then briefly at each other
before walking off in the dark their separate ways
it is surely good to have you in our party lad
said Henry through the last of his happy tears

the cameleers too
by the time we reached our destination
were not complete strangers to me
one of them who's name I cannot recall was quite younger
spoke more in English than his two comrades
but all were kind to the new lad I was
and perhaps because a child they offered every courtesy

each morning when I awoke
for the several days of that first Kallara journey
the younger fellow brought around a hot sweet tea to all
and in this I was included
a spicy lovely thing it was too
the older Afghans broadly smiling at my positive first reaction
once I took the courage of that first sip a cheer was raised

the country was harsh
doubly so in those years of dry
not so far adrift as the crow flies
from the regular old route with the cart
though hugging the river closely
and so in many places quite wooded
fringing endless stretches of olive saltbush and an ochre-pink sandy earth

not too far into the journey
I'd walk rather than ride at the back of the wagon
my young legs able to keep pace for a time
so used I was to that form of travel
and so harsh the boards became on a young rear end
Sam and Theo came to invite me up front too
though a tight squeeze it was the place to be

they laughed at my fear of the height
when first I climbed right up on board
at least double that when atop our old water cart
soon accustomed though to the sway and the view all around
smiles from them both as I mentioned how different it all seemed
like Mr Mac was saying do you recall
up here you really can see the curve of the earth

you get a finer sense of the camels up here an' all
commented Sam to make me laugh
the smell was really something in the heat
with their rear ends right in front to greet us
a smell like any beast something distinctly their own
pungent at times to say the very least
a dusty smelly procession with no shortage of flies to accompany

arriving then at Kallara was way beyond my expectations
more like a small town than a single farm
such a number of people emerged forthwith to greet us
I was shown to my room
a single slim affair with a low bed of boards
at the end of a row of the same
Sam indicating that he was in the very next door

I dumped my bedroll and returned to help where I could
taking provisions and tools handed to me
following instructions as to where they should go
the place had its own blacksmith and saddlery
a store and huge kitchen besides
within that first hour there a dozen or so other hands I met
all going about their tasks earnestly

after the trip of some days up river from town
through the arid terrain that there abounds
we suddenly came upon all this
a million acre run
with the central homestead and surrounds
an entity all its own
such an achievement in itself those days away out there

no sooner had we arrived and the extensive goods unloaded
did the Afghan team start preparing for the return journey
wool bales freshly stamped and waiting
a fraction I was told of what Kallara Station had in store
but they could wait no longer for that drought to end
for a steamer to once again arrive
some at least had to be sold and some income therefore derived

no chance for farewells to those cameleers
though across subsequent years I did better get to know
having in mind as a boy that first time
to quiz them about Grace and her father
yet this never really properly occurred
no details were known to me or anyone
just a sense of sad unease

the team was loaded and early one morning
these fellows new to me just melted away
back down river was the plan so I heard
beyond Wilcannia too if there were still no rain
to Wentworth where there was at least still some Murray flow
a fair undertaking in anyone's language
a hard physical test for beasts and men

and yet that was the thing
it was such a physical world back in those times
we walked everywhere
and even when upon the back of a horse
it too was a fair undertaking for all
not just a step into an automobile no sir
so much of the everyday had physical effort attached

perhaps too that is why it all grabbed me straight away
that life out there on the land
looking back I was such a lost little soul
then the good fortune being thrown into that life so busy
no time to ponder my sadness
instead bolted on to a team all having a go
and needing each other in that isolated station oasis

*

from the start I busied myself with any task assigned
a few months passed and the winter seemed suddenly to loom
that awful dry would be some years before breaking
though we were not to know it then
yet as grim as it was for us on that drained river there
we were far better off than most
due in no small part to the intelligence and compassion of my hosts

intelligence most obviously in the management
from the brothers Station whose run it was
right through to the managers I got to know
including the young Mr Mac and his Uncle Jim
and compassion with it too by and large
their ability to look at life through the eyes of their fellow man
then actively show some care

then on top of the dry a world depression was on
the Australian Mortgage and Finance Company
the only mob making hay
perhaps at the heart of the problems back then
was the confidence from those mostly good years
as people spoke of the 1870s and 80s
hence places stocked to the brim when drought did come

then add a rabbit swarm and you have a calamity ready made
far more than the earth could bare
and like any drought impossible to see an end
when the camp fire's colours are reflected in each evening sky
and every morning you awake to another dry dawn
the earth fragile so vast and so ancient both
was crumbling and being blown away

it will rain again Master Jack
have no fear of that
this long dry though
just the earth's way of telling us something
that she is in need of rest
and especially so
in hard times such as this

so Jack Quayle said
and such a figure he became in my young life
not so many weeks into my time there
Jack arrived in his smart buggy and horse team besides
welcomed by all hands and managers too
came like a breeze of positivity
he and Hannah his wife with a young family all smiles

until then I had of course mixed with many Paarkintji out there
such was Kallara's reputation it seemed
to treat people well
offer what work there was
despite the season folk seemed to come and go
a kind of hub as it were for work and some extra sustenance
away from the grog and unease of the towns

yet it was Jack Quayle
who became my true window
my connection to Aboriginal people there
and in a different way to Grace and her mum
who were now such a part of town
Jack a Paarkintji man though raised by a squatter of note
Hannah also raised in both white and traditional ways

perhaps because I was just a lad
and like me though named John people mostly called him Jack
or maybe to do with being alone and still young
for whatever reason he befriended me whenever there
as I saw him be with others
showing kindness from the very first day
and it was impossible not to show respect to him

such a figure he cut too compared to all other black and white
athletic and upon a horse tall
in the best boots and attire I had seen
stock whip in hand straight of back looking grand
he would shoot me a look before heading off somewhere
above the grandest and thickest of any black beard
as if to say *this is me and here I do belong*

Jack's importance in those times
I think cannot be overstated
and that of Hannah too
me just a boy could see the strength that they contained
a foot firmly and strongly in their own rich culture and ways
speaking their language naturally and with pride
yet a foot too in the English world they seemed willing to stride

it was through Jack too
that over time I got to know more of the Aboriginal stockmen
not to mention his children and others close to my age
in those years some families lived in a camp nearby
the men moving between stations
at least across those few runs able to support the dispossessed
enabling some work even in such a dry

an exceptional horseman
a breaker of renown
Jack could turn his hand it seemed to anything
so at home out on that land
a quiet leader of such capacity
he and Hannah both had the respect of all
working up and down the Darling and the Corner Country besides

Mr Mac too you could tell enjoyed his company
always keen to learn from the stockman barely his senior in age
and I too was asked to assist with them both
out checking stock or the ground tanks
it seemed that every bore we came to
was the result of Jack's labours anyways
the impact of the man was clear

what then of you young Jack why you suddenly out this way
I was greatly surprised at his question
showing interest in a young white boy
interest in how I came to be there
on land clearly part of his body and soul
Mr Mac was with us also
making me wonder if discussions already had been had

my answer was perhaps unsurprisingly
wrapped with caution and not a little grief
I had after all quite a few weighty things
sitting on my shoulders but twelve years old
the father of a good friend
my best friend Grace's dad
introduced me as he knows Mr Mac here

and clearly expecting to hear more of a yarn Jack continued
so who your family
where they at then
I kept busying myself with the work I'd started
before his first question had come
sweeping up some chaff I'd spilled at the stables just before
hoping that Mr Mac would explain but no he also waited for me

until just a few months ago
with my dad we had a water cart
between town and White Cliffs mostly
yet he died suddenly just at the end of the year gone
my mother too passed on yet I was not much more than a babe
have no recollection of her face
just a photo that is still stuck on that water cart

I was given a few moments of silence before Jack's response
never did meet your father boy
that road there you talk of
too many grog shanties for me and close to town
things I try to avoid
but I have heard his good name mentioned around
and so sad the way he died

at this both men became silent
perhaps noticing the upset it caused
they moved towards Jack's tents pitched just beyond the yards
to return some time later
my work finished I was happy to stay at the stable door
observing the horses at rest
so calming they were to me especially if dark thoughts came my way

hey there Jack
announced Jack Quayle
Mr Mac and I must in the morning go out along the north fence line
fancy then riding with us beside
I jumped down from the stable rail
barely containing my glee
thank you Mr Quayle I must have fairly beamed as he scruffed my hair

there'd be countless rides taken subsequently
during my time out there
yet none so clear in my memory as those two days
Mr Mac had chosen a quiet pony for me
while both men sat astride horses of a stature befitting them
though they could surely have ridden as swift as the wind
they were very patient all the while coaxing me along

though I had of course been with horses all my life
Parkes being the most notable one
I had ridden precious little until then
yet in such company did I feel soon born to it
their casual tuition and encouragement a fine thing
we did check a huge long fence line true
but a ride and a long yarn was also the intent of these two young men

a fine thing it was to strike out in that small group
my first real excursion very far from the Government House
as the main hub of the station was called
and as the heat of summer had long gone
the days were then not so harsh
a typically fresh crisp morning start
the clearest of days they were

the plan was to ride up river a way
before striking out along the boundary
west we would go to a certain point
camp the night then return the next day via a series of earth tanks
I had strapped on my bedroll as instructed
in truth still everything that I did own
the two men carried all else including rifles at their sides

coo-hee won't you lad emphasised Mr Mac early on
if you even think you see a pig or a dog
not just for sport either I'll add
I'd be keen to dispatch some on any day
and before long there were signs of plenty of both
the carcass of several mauled sheep in a row
and the rough ploughing of the already troubled earth in patches large

amid one stretch particularly broad
Jack stopped his horse quite suddenly
just look how far this all goes
must be a fair mob of them gettin' around
for men so positive it was a strange thing to see
despair in the eyes of both
as they scanned the dishevelled ground

it's not just the pigs should be shot
but whatever damn fool who first let them run free
I'd be happy to align with my sights
declared Mr Mac as we began to move beyond the destroyed ground
not long before Jack responded with both wit and a barb
well at least if from only your rifle then
all blackfellas will be safe from harm

we saw more examples too
the devastation of pigs gone wild
not to mention of course the very serious disaster
that was the introduced humble rabbit
in some places during those years
it was as if the ground moved before your very eyes
such was their staggering population

one small blessing in all this
was that there was another economy that could arise
a ready source of protein was there
even if lamb beef or roo were deemed superior
in such extreme dry times it was a handy back-stop to hunger
not to mention the pelts at three pennies a pair
many men earning more than they ever had before

that evening in fact
Jack disappeared while Mr Mac and I built a fire
just two shots were fired not a long distance from us
and two furry carcasses were there for us to share
the meat done on the coals and washed down with plenty of tea
the evening was ripe for conversation
and those two young men of ambition did not disappoint me

perhaps here's a way
for this young fellow to get busy
what do you say Jack
turn this lad into our chief rabbit man
in reply Jack Quayle smiled through his rich beard
could be just the very thing
and he should have work until an old man

I didn't know of course then
how much indeed the rabbit would later become
such a bonus to me and my little family
some years down the track
as it was for many of course
almost the saviour of many country towns
that little furry curse

that evening though many things were talked through
and I have seen this often since
how people are more inclined to speak their minds true
when in a circle around a fire
something so simple about it
makes everyone there feel the same
even a lad of twelve felt more equal to the men when staring at the same flames

equity it was too that formed the main thrust of their conversation
I found it astounding really
Mr Mac and Jack both
from such vastly different backgrounds
could have ideas about so many things
that aligned almost seamlessly
two men of such capacity

the weather I know Mr Mac began
is of course beyond our control
this dry cannot be blamed on anyone
yet there is an argument to call to account
those who have exploited this land thus far in seasons good
and there have been plenty of them so it seems
with no thought of such lean times as these

it was a theme to which I heard both men often return
an almost fury at those from barely a generation before
first European settlers or those immediately after
who despite their hardships significant
had at least the benefit of several years of decent rain
as a lad I knew nothing more and so agreed with all they said
yet I have noted such talk from many since of the failings of those coming before

perhaps I am too harsh Mr Mac further explained
yet it has to be said
that not a mile of thought
was employed by most
during those good good years
we would still have it hard now let me say straight
but with less greed it may have been a better deal just now I truly feel

sentiments to which Jack Quayle readily agreed
greed is the word there right there
Mr Mac you speak true
and not just on these pastures no
overstocked so
but the river too
our lifeblood this 'ere Paarka treated so badly badly

so true Jack so true continued Mr Mac calm yet serious
have ye heard of the weir then
the weir now built up at Bourke
not only has the flow become swift
with the removal of any and all
but that weir will hold water for them well and good
yet what about us here downstream

I had to query them then
what was this talk of a weir
and Jack too I recall
with the description given by Mr Mac
drawn in the dirt
by the light of that fine ember fire
Jack then walked a little away quiet for a time

so do you mean to tell me then
he began upon his return
that not only are you fellas 'ere
strippin' this country bare with your sheep
lettin' every rabbit en pig 'ave its share
leavin' nothin' but dust
in these dry years that will always come around

not only are ye happy
for all that te come te bear
but also too
ye now know somethin'
of holdin' water back for ye greed
let it drain through without snags for the steamers
and then dam it up elsewhere for your purpose

his anger was spoken to Mr Mac
yet it was not he who was the true target
Mr Mac said not a word
but nodded in acquiescence
looked only at the fire and at me calmly
with perhaps both shame and understanding
but that steady tirade from Jack Quayle was a powerful thing

these dry times such as now
are a thing natural to here
and the low often has always been
that is the cycle of things for how many generations
but with all the marshes being drained
and logs and snags removed for them boats
there's nothin' to hold the water when it does rain

our Paarka is gonna look like a drain
nothin' but a drain
instead of the series of slow pools it used to be
mad isn't it
building weirs now to hold back the flow
when there was weirs natural all along and cared for
all these centuries gone

the conversations went on quite long I recall
that clear cool evening around the fire
and on the morning that followed I awoke before the men
just at the first breath of dawn
deciding to gather a little more wood
the fire ash but with warmth still below to rekindle
I attempted to leave without rousing my senior companions

and of all the matters large and small
that my mind could possibly retain through the years
I still so vividly recall
that one three-cornered-jack at dawn
the thorns and burrs in that arid country are many
but that little fellow half an inch or more from barb to barb
hard as nails and needle sharp was a thing

straight through my bare foot it went
as I stood to reach down for my boots
the cool fine pink dirt is a nice touch on bare skin
but that thorn was designed for pain purely
it is perhaps something I remember still
for the large gasp not to leave my lips
anxious that my companions continue their troubled slumber

I succeeded
and even after removing the problem thorn
a thick dot of blood and a deep bruise to greet the day
even with boots on
was I for several hours reminded of that single needle
yet I struck out regardless to gather wood
with a dawn ever clear advancing

I had worried before that evening
before hearing the anxieties of Mr Mac and Jack Quayle
the earth I had looked upon with some concern
even for a boy as I was
a long drought was an obvious thing
a force to accentuate even further
your already clear insignificance within the world

yet the words from the night before
had solidified some ideas in me
caused me new concerns from what I'd heard
and sharpened my already established fears
it was as if I had new eyes that morning
appreciative all the more
of the only landscape I had ever known

there was no need to walk far
to gather a few pieces of dry wood of varying size
but I wandered off none the less
just enjoying the cool while it lasted
following without any purpose
the imprints in the soft bare soil
the arrow marks of an emu

a small mob of roos placidly watched me go by
the stiff olive inverted brooms of saltbush
providing shelter of sorts
throughout either the hot day or dark night
for that family and so many more
their calm a contrast to the subsequent explosion of pounding
as my boots came upon rabbits more than a few

maybe that would be a purpose for me
as Jack had suggested
hunting the rabbit
at least doing some small good
ridding the land of one pest
at least as well as I could
tilting at windmills though it may be

returning to the camp
to quietly rebuild flame from the ash
Jack was the first to wake
Mr Mac sleeping solid through our conversation for a while
positive was Jack Quayle upon hearing my morning resolution
to rid the rabbit from the land
smiling though he no doubt was too at my youthful naivete

there is some talk
Jack returned without warning
to my father's tale
of the need for the water cart or not nowadays
I have myself sunk more than one bore out that way with various teams
since the first hole dropped right on Kallara here
a few years already now people using whatever lies underneath

and along that track more and more
sad to say but those bores
they become another excuse for some lair
to erect some form of grog shanty
and White Cliffs itself surely
has need of far more than a few of Furphy's tanks
of the cart such as you and your father hauled

so I can understand why such talk
that the real cargo ain't about water
a cart may in fact carry a different kind of wealth
and at this Jack paused a while
close to me he was
letting me work on the fire myself
not interfering but also observing my reactions

yet I could not respond
even though no question had truly been asked
I had no comment in truth to add
but Jack's simple observations that morning
did cause me more than a touch of anxiety
concluding he did with *some say your father carried things to help others along*
while other carts may be less noble

my mind naturally became for some time an emotional swirl
there being some element of truth in what Jack Quayle had to say
memories of things half seen between my father and others
packages carried in the long drawer beneath the cart seat
a near anger unusual for him
if I ever lingered there
and of course thoughts of Grace and her father and things half seen

the journey back that next morning a much quieter affair
I with my thoughts
Jack always with his and a keen quiet eye scanning the land
only Mr Mac as we checked the second or third and last tank
began to query what he called my almost sullen mood
and I replied with honesty
that Jack had earlier made me question some memories

it was only then that I heard of their views
Mr Mac seeming to know also of what Jack Quayle had heard
keen they were to several times throughout clearly state
that my father was held by them and many
in the highest regard
things outside the law perhaps
but things that were just and good

I mentioned of course the Chinese at White Cliffs
how they had scared Grace so much
that last night we were there
news which was greeted by my companions
with nodding confirmation of the tales they had heard
of a man who plied diligently his water trade
yet thought it wrong how the Chinese were treated

my father I had seen
befriend them over the years
open as he was in his own quiet way
to any and all
he would speak to an Indian hawker pulled up
in the same manner as to a white man in the finest gig
or for that matter the likes of Jack Quayle

this country though at those times
and it is something to remember clear
at the very time of such talk and planned celebrations
of the colonies becoming one federated thing
though it contained people of many tongues and shades
they were only allowed step ashore
if their purpose suited that of those in charge

Federation was a fine thing indeed
yet in this country of many cultures
which we were even way back then
seems to me the purpose of federating
was to suit only the ends of those in charge
much more than a welcome to all
laws and rights sat only with white men

yet good people there have been
in any age of man
brave too as Mr Mac and Jack Quayle would repeatedly describe
my father and such as he
carrying within his cart as they believed and heard say
small parcels of opals
for his Chinese friends and perhaps even Afghans too

the traders at the diggings
or in Wilcannia and further afield
all white men and mostly of German stock
would rarely if ever hazard such a trade
yet if my father acted for them
pieces large or small would become a legal currency
and no doubt benefit all

I had seen things I did admit
close I was to my father
often there had been times
when Chinese fellows would see our wagon and I thought just say hello
and in all honesty I am yet to see
packages large or small be exchanged
but that is not to say my father could this have easily concealed

a kind of pride in him I remember sweeping over me
that I still sense even now looking back
and though I have no hard proof of his deeds
legal or otherwise
misguided or just
my father had done what he thought right despite the times
likely even paying for it with his life

before our return to the stables that day
Mr Mac had also quizzed me about Old Tom
in the weeks following my father's death
questions were being asked of this famously surly man
more than most others happy to open displays
anger verbal and physical at anyone less than white
beneath it all the rage at the Afghan impinging on his bullocky trade

Jack Quayle too mentioned this unsavoury man
met him at Dry Lake skiting he was about he had a potion too
that could cause the death of any man
spitting profanities about the Chinese
then Afghans and all who wished to befriend them
fearful and protecting his own little bullock team
awful man so full up with hate

I of course to them described
my encounter and memory of the same
Grace's dad and Old Tom almost coming to blows
if not for my father's intervention
grog of course involved
news that gave them no surprise
some men though said Jack Quayle *were bad even without the grog*

*

it would be quite a few months after
the end of that year
the first day of the next it was
the first day of January 1901
when I would see Old Tom once more
alone I was mostly too
on that picnic day to mark the country's Inauguration

still no rain and no sign of any by then
no show of joining the celebrations at Wilcannia by boat
Mr Mac had asked me to join the small party from Kallara
travelling down the dusty river track in the two best wagons
the journey doubled as a chance to also pick up more supplies
but all were keen to be there in time for the actual day of Federation
or Inauguration as it were often referred

there was some form of a solemn ceremony I recall
outdoors it was and a hot dry day
may have been by the river but I cannot rightly bring it to mind
anyways a variety of celebrations there were
known it was that on that day
a huge gathering in Sydney's Centennial Park
would be echoed by picnics and parties across the land

we were to have our first Prime Minister
Sir Edmund Barton's name and that of Henry Parkes too
fairly thick in the air
colourful bunting and decorations of all description
the town did look a bit special as we entered
after a long journey beside a river so dry
we camped two nights or maybe it was three

from the first minute was I also scanning the streets for Grace
though no sign of her
all the music and dancing she would have so loved
and for me I had myself convinced
that I'd again be a part of her laughter
but no she was nowhere to be seen
the magical music making here and there seeming sad without my friend

Old Tom however was most definitely there
his long thin frame and rough beard a steady sight
at any makeshift bar or grog tent
during those days of celebration
though he did not speak to me
and nor did I have either courage or desire
to raise any questions with he

alone I was for most of that time
and any other visit too with Mr Mac into town
he content for me to wander
a few pennies in my pocket for perhaps some sweets
or some kind of trifle that took my fancy
he would attend to business of various kinds
and happily too I learned this included one of the merchant's daughters

I was even asked to dinner
with Mr Mac and some of his friends I did not know
a fair celebration it truly was
closing that first day of Federation
the household had children
but just as at Kallara all a bit younger than me
and town kids with somehow different ways

we sat and ate on the wide verandas we children
I with them though for so many months by then
had I been working as a man
yet we could see through the window and hear
the happy gathering with no shortage of food and good cheer
glasses raised to toast Queen and country
and no doubt to Mr Barton our first Prime Minister

embarrassed a bit I was too
as I couldn't escape the feeling
that it was the same sandstone home
not far from the court house as it was
that I had with Grace that night so happily
danced to music by the roses in the dark
if not the exact place I felt her memory just the same

thinking about it though
she would more than likely not have been welcomed
not of the right colour for that particular party
Mr Mac through the window beaming
across the table was a young woman with his full attention
Clara he spoke of for many a day
Clara he hoped to persuade up river to come

the journey home
up along that river without flow
included tales of the special celebrations
and apart from descriptions of Clara's beauty
Mr Mac could also tell me
his brief encounter with the contrasting ugliness
that was Old Tom

on the first evening there
Mr Mac had done as he always in town tried to do
met up with some acquaintances
at one of the several hotels
when in walks Old Tom
already in that early evening
clearly cut half through with grog

a figure of mockery Mr Mac outlined
asked soon to move on by the publican
at which he cursed back something fierce
a constable finally moving him along
then after he'd departed all spoke the same
all acquaintances good working men from various large runs
had heard he'd killed more than one man had that Old Tom

an angrier more bitter man
young Jack I am yet to meet
ten years now I have been out here
not much more than you when I arrived
hoping to make my way somehow my good family left behind
and it is true so true what that say of those of this Outside land as it be called
good men here are magnificent and the bad be very bad

a hard thing it would be to prove
that Old Tom was behind your father's demise
yet from everything I have seen and heard
he would certainly have such a deed within him
a bad man if ever there walked
and though your dear father may have been of humble means
for his honest deeds well magnificent would be a better description

Mr Mac then said something
some nice words that preceded a long silence between he and I
and though I never met your father
I know him to be a truly good man
for I know his son
even now I find myself gasping at these words from years ago
surprised and proud I was for them to come to me from such a fellow

*

there were of course other times
I had opportunity to get to Wilcannia again
yet despite my best endeavours
no end of asking and searching
all came to nought in the end
their house abandoned when I called during those Federation days
gone to Menindee or somewhere that way was all I could learn of Grace

that return to Kallara in 1901
to be honest was difficult for a time
so sure I was that I would again see my good friend
someone my age and dear to me
the great celebrations of so many all around
jarred a little with a boy trying to become a man
wondering how he may make his way in that harsh dry world

with the drought continuing as if without end
there was an anxiety of sorts
even from one so positive as Mr Mac
his thoughts would sometimes be exposed
little wool was the reality
and many a surrounding run did not survive
he was just an employee after all

even the brothers Station
owners of some means it was said as Mr Mac explained
astute though they were
a hard time of it those days surely for all
a flock of tens of thousands reduced to just a fraction
plus the pressure from this new nation
for closer settlement yet again

the big runs as they were known
a million or so acres apportioned to just one man
was good only for a time it seemed
then on top of the drought and the depression of the 1890s
there was of course the rabbit plague
plague it became known and sure that's what it be
in many parts nothing short of devastation

yet for a lad such as me
and many older and even whole families
the feral rabbit was a godsend true
terrible that may sound to now say
though far from prime lamb
it did sustain many bellies both humble and grand
and those pelts were a market ready made

my tasks around the whole property were varied
and cheap labour as a boy my place perhaps secure
unlike so many who had to be let go
even Henry and Sam my other allies
for a time also took to the track with their swags
returning only after the rains in 1903
finally did start to come our way

in the one week I may have done just the same dull task
or perhaps all manner of things
help with a fence or cleaning out a dry tank
even in the kitchen with cook
or help Mr Soo if he let me in his miraculous Chinese vegetable garden
Kallara was a small self contained thing
though in those days diminished in number

it was with the bunnies though
I did feel like it was somehow my own show
a dozen traps at first Mr Mac set me up
never letting me repay him
and out I would go each evening to set the sprung metal jaws
and before dawn each day would I rouse
so eager to check the rewards

the heat and the dry too much at times for even they
especially I guess in those last months before the wet
dead I would find them
dead stretched out alone
or in clumps in the dust
emaciated beneath the scorching sun
or like desert flotsam half buried after a wild dust storm

and lord do I remember that early morning when the rain did come
a series of very hot days there had been
yet clouds started to build that final evening before
not that this always translated to relief from the skies
dark still when I awoke but it was clear in the air
a rich clear smell of distant rain
a swiftness in my legs to get to my pony before the storm

Mr Barton
I had been urged by Mr Mac to name him
once he'd heard the story of Parkes
my father's gelding
and a lovely small colt he was too
with me almost till I went away
Mr Barton almost made it to 1915

that morning heading out he was a lively young thing
though he took me to where I needed to go
in the first bare light setting off
a track leading a mile or so away
weaving on soft ochre between mulga and saltbush
to the series of warrens in a slight rocky rise
the metal sound of rabbits wounded and caught joined by a thunder roll

if I had been upon him I may well have ended on the ground
born only a year or so before
Mr Barton knew nothing of the smells or sounds of rain
he ran scared for a time
but thankfully returned to my side
perhaps also through fear
allowing me to load the traps and dead pairs before leading him home

we were soon to feel the rain too
coming in a rush before reaching proper shelter
I did wonder what that young horse may think
cool and heavy in drops large it did come down
for me also it was quite the novelty
a young boy was I when last there had been such a storm
sheltering with my father beneath our small water cart

Kallara was of course a happy place to which to return that early morning
everyone celebrating the rain
Mr Mac still in his night shirt with feet bare
rushing over to Mr Soo in the garden
gazing at puddles already forming
difficult is was to distinguish on every face
the moisture of rain or happy tears unfolding

that clutch of rabbits also
did not that morning smell the same
dry they had been when at the traps I cracked their necks
but once saturated on the journey home
the usual pale brown and grey of their fur
was a much darker and pungent thing
and slippery when it came to the stripping

and how the land lifted
within days it seemed
a carpet of new grasses and flowers
seeds dormant in the dust
at least those not blown away in so many a bad dry storm
leapt to life so wondrously
rabbits they also flourished again I could soon feel in the fur

while the river too
slow at first
but then following some good solid rains
upstream as required in Queensland
did reach a good flow once more
and such a fine thing too
a full banking flow pulsing through

leads a man to wonder
Mr Mac suggested as we checked the height of the flow
just how much more there would be here
if not for that Bourke weir
and indeed if it were once again as when Jack Quayle described
all along right up and downstream
snags and marshes holding onto whatever comes

the next visit I recall
of the great Jack Quayle
was some weeks at least beyond those initial rains
and even after the best of the river rise
the water having come down from way up in Queensland
already mostly surged on through
he didn't say much but his disgust was clear

a right drain it become
this mighty river
just bleeds right out now see
like a beast felled with a severed limb
the strong fighting pulse
at first with the rains it still has
but so soon now without a fight the beat dims

so spoke Jack Quayle
his wife Hannah by his side
serious yet calm as ever
in the same fine rig and several horses
their little ones growing I suggested
at which he again scruffed my hair
suggesting I too were a bit closer to being a young man

in any company I had been
in my limited experience at that time
they were two people who commanded respect
a clear eyed sober dignity
a compassion for all
so knowledgeable and hardworking
so much wisdom beyond their years

my view of them has not once dimmed
instead in the years intervening
having learned quite some more
of the hardships they would have faced
like any out that way in those days
but exacerbated simply because of their race
they are the examples our history should honour and record

you mentioned often your friend Grace
Jack Quayle said quite suddenly to me
nice it is to have a friend a good friend
even if you don't see them for a time
it will still be good when you do
she is safe and at Weinteriga Station on the Menindee Road
just so you know

as Mr Mac listened intently
and as Hannah came forward with a huge smile
I had to force myself to breathe
Jack Quayle laughing aloud at my ill ease
my obvious happiness just on hearing the name
then with a hand outstretched
Hannah offered a small parcel of rough white cloth

we've been down that way a while
a bit of work for Jack Quayle the famous breaker
triggering laughs from both her husband and Mr Mac
over time Grace and her mum mentioned this young fella
the water cart and such things as your dear father
then so once she realised the connection with us up here
I tell ye there was no stopping the smiles

and this as we left
she has trusted us to give to her friend
there is another similar
belonging to her
to make the pair
both coming her mother explained to me
from that Hector but that's all she would say

my hands I am sure were trembling
accepting the small parcel
corners tied quite tight and some time ago
no doubt by Grace's long slim hands
finally released to reveal
a small pale stone no bigger than a three-cornered burr
but with enough flecks to reveal its treasure

crikey Jack
you have something there
Mr Mac said encouragingly
there's a treasure right enough
in more than one way a little treasure
I said not a word for some time
just gazed at it and held to the light against that pale blue sky

the stone's connection for my friend Grace and I Hannah further explained
all young Grace and her mum would say
was that Hector
the man who'd been with her
since she with child to an Afghan man
that Hector had been told of Old Tom
met him at several camps along the ways

in any case the rotten skeleton of Old Tom was found
and these things and more were in his possession
there was much talk that two of his victims
Grace's dad some Afghan man and your honest father
your father who maybe helped some Chinese with their stones
knowing this it made sense to all
that these things stolen should in some way be returned

a fair silence both happy and sad there ensued
Mr Mac however offered all he too knew
I think you know young Jack there has been talk of such perfidy
from hawkers and swaggies and other carriers of yarns
of that fellow having something to do with your father's passing
and that of at least another besides
so as sad it may be there are some whose demise we needn't mourn

and there was also not so long before
word that a team of bullocks
one pair still joined in their yoke
were found wandering up by Wanaaring Bore
no master or sign of one ever to be found thus far
fair to say would it be
that it is of the same death that we speak

Jack Quayle in answering his friend
also came a bit closer to me
taking the stone briefly from my hand
it is logic to say the same
the remains of the man while not the same
were indeed up that way
separated from his wagon and from reason from water and life

you need to know something though young fella
Jack Quayle continued earnestly
it is no small thing
to remove a stone
more often
our people feel
it is the wrong thing in the order of the land

and 'specially so
one of these opal stones here
see though think on this
great value is put upon them
people goin' crazy over White Cliffs you know still now
for all the money they think they may bring
but what is its true value then

those coloured stones have always rested there
our people consider them special too
the Creator when he stepped upon the earth
came as a rainbow
and when 'is foot touch the ground
at what is now called White Cliffs
the ground sparked up and them rainbow colours entered the stones

so that's where those stones should be
placed back there
to restore the balance of things
but this one special for you too eh
'cause your woman got that matching pair
ye girl there waiting with her one of the pair
how 'bout that for special eh

these last words were designed for laughter at my expense
which was forthcoming and long from all
no doubt red faced I defended
she's not my woman
just a friend
triggering more digs about me and she
before Jack Quayle decided to conclude his advice

so this 'ere stone
that from Grace is given to thee
is a treasure truly
and you could have it cut proper
make a quid for sure
to help you on your way
or you may take another path 'ere's me 'oping anyways

treasure it Jack
as a thing from she
apart you two are now
but maybe some day
her stone and yours together will be
and together be returned
to that rainbow ground

the words of Jack Quayle
had a big impact upon me
I determined then and there to keep it safe
promising him so
to one day I did hope with she
place it back in its place
right at least one wrong if I could

*

never did I think though
that the years would progress as they have and swiftly so
Kallara so busy to rebuild some
following the harsh years of the dry
I was pressed into any and all jobs
in the wool shed too of course more and more as I grew
and in any spare time I'd be busy with the rabbits too

and just to cap my exhaustion
usually on a Sunday
when the place gave some token respect to the Sabbath
work slowing if possible somewhat
Mr Mac would be keen to put books in front of me
urging my reading and work with numbers
not to mention trying to mend my still poor writing hand

my father had done his best way before too
scratching out simple words to read
he'd underline words for me to recognise
from one of the weeklies we'd pick up from town
or Wilcannia's own *Western Grazier*
tough I found it but it was at least a start
something upon which Mr Mac could build

a school did exist in those times
but on the track as we were
my attendance was barely none
then when Grace was made not feel welcome
by other white ones and their families
despite her mother's persistence
my father then washed his hands of the whole show it seems

but whatever learning I suppose I did have
like so much else I owe to Mr Mac
in those years before the War he was many things
a real thinker a hard worker
and a compassionate man
my adopted big brother then mentor though my boss
wanting success but with an infectious energy

I guess it was in the woolshed I most remember his capacity
in those few good years we did have
sheep everywhere it seemed to me
shearers and so many other hands
yet from the far paddocks right through to the wool press
stamping the bales and seeing them loaded on a steamer or camel train
Mr Mac kept all the parts moving and with the quiet respect of all

busy as he was
he still had time to sit with a youth such as me
urging me to raise my eyes to the horizon
think beyond Kallara to what my life might be
as much as I do love this place too
he said more than once as I recall it
don't be afraid to think beyond these lovely smoothed lanolin boards

Jack Quayle knew his value too I figure
arriving especially to farewell his friend in 1915
when it was known Mr Mac was heading to the War
quite the news it then was
questions raised about how we would all get along
without the calm clever head
of that totally capable young man

I had said my own farewells
promising to be there soon too
either in Europe or someplace else
on the far side of the globe
I was sure we would meet one day
and with more excitement than fear
he walked to the stables in civilian clothes

Mr Quayle was there to greet him alone
and though I have no idea of their words
both men smiled but very solemnly
and it was a handshake long and quite profound
Mr Mac lifted his hat to all before on his way
the very picture of a man in his prime as they say
yet the last time we saw him alive

he had not wooed his Clara
so committed to Kallara was he
and she to town and thereafter the city of Adelaide
some pain that caused him too
beneath his relentless positivity
there was at times a quiet fellow
whose thoughts were purely his own

no sooner had our common friend galloped away
did Mr Jack Quayle come over to me
if this country had a few more fellas like that one there
well a good place it surely would be
he turned on his fine leather boot heels
straight back to his tent
his small tidy wagon too set once again beyond the stable and yards

then just on dark that same evening
at my room did Jack Quayle appear
tomorrow being Sunday
and the river with a fresh coming through
what say we cast a line or two
an invitation to which I readily agreed
I'll knock on you then at dawn instructed he

there were fish aplenty that day too
a corner with a deep pool and some overhangs
Jack Quayle thought it best and I followed
though for each yellow belly I pulled in
my companion would have hauled in three
both of us pretty quiet
melancholy for sure at the thought of our absent friend

walking the horses home though I recall some words
a net with a catch of a dozen or more
lay across Jack Quayle's chestnut mare
like a funny kind of damp saddle bag
that old Ngatji must be happy today
that there river spirit wouldn't be givin' up all these
not unhappily anyways

he asked if the war was where I too would soon go
it seems like the right thing to do I suggested
it seems like a stupid English nightmare to me replied he
and as it happened of course
as it transpired those next few years
I was wrong and he was right
a nightmare like no other

there was no debating the matter then however
my mind was clear as was his
and it has since long been proved
that I was not alone in my naivete
what sticks with me though
from that afternoon slow meander along the loamy river bank
had nothing to do with war

you did mention one time
this quietly strong man began
something precious to you was no longer yours
a photo you no longer had
do you recall the first time we met
you but a boy
thrown up this way after you lost your dad

I did remember but couldn't believe that so did he
a photo of my mother that would be
you don't mean to tell me
but then Jack Quayle intervened
no no sorry lad
not my meaning to raise your hopes
but many a year ago I did have a search for thee

he then explained
not long after our first meeting
despite his distaste for the place
the mining and the grog everywhere
he found himself in White Cliffs anyways
chasing some work back in those dry hard years
and remembering the lost treasure of a grieving boy

I couldn't find it
sad to say
but I did try just so you know
found what I presumed was your father's water cart wagon
safe at the back of the pub there at that time
not hard it was to sneak a look
most others thereabouts busy with rum

the whole cart looked bare
then I lifted the seat back
accidentally I found it to be on a hinge
and there beneath a thin little drawer
a place for treasures nothing surer thought I
but nothing there
nothing for me to find and bring to thee

not for the first time
had this man surprised me
with simple generosity
a shame I have nothing for you now
yet I too have none of my old people
no images to look upon
yet they are always with me I truly feel

Mr Mac too had tried to help me I then explained
way back then at about that same time
offering to visit the humble home
shared in Wilcannia by my father and I
no need I explained as all things important were upon the wagon
yet he went just the same on one visit thereafter
returning with a box of clothes cleared out way before by the landlord

small things it were true
treasures such as that rough stone from Grace I held dear
or memories of my father
watching him content
camped at his favourite place out on the track
or him showing me just now and then
that special portrait he'd held so dear

maybe it's just me an old fool now
looking back nostalgically
romantically you could even say
days long past can assume a certain rosy glow
yet it both warms me and it pains me to recollect now
proud and happy am I to have known such men
but sorry too that after that day we did not meet again

the War of course did consume me for several years
after which to a different life I returned
and though I was out that way some times
our paths never did seem to collide
so instead I have to treasure Jack Quayle's final words to me
go steady and strong then good young Jack
and keep that lucky stone close to your heart

*

my years there though the work was constant and hard
was nothing short of a treasure for me
I went to Kallara as a lad
knowing nothing of very much at all
and I left a young man
prepared more than most
for that awful thing called war

I'll speak not of that life here
tales of carnage and boredom are not the memories I wish to share
that may become another yarn
if I feel down the track that it's in me
but when looking over a life
your own or any other
it's the good and the powerful things surely most worthy of recollection

one thing from that World War I should though share
an object that made me smile
was the old trusty water cart also pressed into service
a Furphy it also had to be
a lifeblood amid carnage and suffering
and a sure place to pick up a yarn
and if embellished well then all the better for the thirst

upon my return I applied for something I never thought would be
my own little patch of ground
thanks to Billy Hughes and his Soldier Settler scheme
much maligned too it came to be
enough fellows thrived but more it seems failed
there were no big runs in those times given away
hard it was anywhere but for me a true godsend

from all my young orphaned years
working land on all sorts of tasks
I knew something of hardship
knew drought and flood both
so those five years of government obligation post-war
conditions and loans to repay
were things possible for me and with at first only myself to feed

beyond Narromine was my good fortune
just 532 acres but fair water and decent ground
not the wonderful size of Kallara no
but enough of that big western sky for me
and still I call it home
and in years when I had to seek it
I've never been short of work elsewhere

lucky I was too
to meet someone who'd put up with me and my ways
Meg my lovely wife of a local family out that way
we had our boy before long and what joy for several years
but then the twins came
our girls
who never once got to breathe that clear western air

dying at birth
and with them
the smile of beautiful Meg
the doctors said it was from the complications of labour that we lost her
but I know it was from a broken heart
so it was just our boy Ewan and I
ignorant of the parallels I was not

wanting to be there for my lad
not taken away as my mother and father both had been from me
he became my world entirely
watching him grow into a successful man such pride I had never known
steady job he had too with the bank
but then of course war again began to loom
farewelling him well that was the hardest day of all

walking back from the station
to the suddenly silent home
I remembered a story once heard
about a mother grieving
in Sydney so I think it was following The Great War
story goes that alone she mourned for her son who had been taken
she would simply not accept that he was gone

each evening no matter what the weather offered
alone she walked the long streets to the station
expect him to step from a train
a tragic sight for all
who daily watched her tears
neighbours giving up consoling her madness
over that train that never came

Ewan did return
and now with a babe of his own
living in Dubbo not an hour away
how lucky can one man like me be
honestly
a grandfather
how can this fortune have come to be

and then the luckiest of all things occurred
I met an old friend once more
a picnic race day
dragged along by Ewan
just after he took his Dubbo position
a year or more ago now
how the world does turn around

the extended party and shin-dig afterwards
something akin to a gathering of the clans
for black and white and all breeds between
protesting before though I was
determined that my dancing days were behind me
then a woman sitting across the tables
had a face I surely knew

yet I'd had that feeling before
through the years in all sorts of places
thinking it was Grace's smile in a crowd
only to be disappointed and feel like a fool
trying to grasp at memories
the mists of youth I would reprimand myself
when she may well not even have been alive

but that evening was something again
Grace a woman near me suddenly said quite loudly
come over and meet my daughter
she did so and I must have looked a right goose indeed
frozen I was and just staring at her
so much so that Grace also began looking at me
and then amid a gasp and a hug and not a few tears we found ourselves reunited

I had some explaining to do
with my son and daughter-in-law
yet all was good before long
Grace and I sat and spoke into the wee hours
we always were the best of friends
we just didn't see each other for fifty or so years
it was just as Jack Quayle told me way back then

even if you don't see them for a while
it will be good when you do
yet it was beyond good
seeing her face right there
two old fools holding hands
me alive as if with new lungs
not wanting the evening to end

I offered a concise history or sorts
of the so many years intervening
and Grace of course had quite a tale to tell
three children though she had lost another two
married to a man from Menindee Mission
he died of a stroke *didn't drink but smoked like we all did*
she said waving her thin lined hands

a hard worker a good man
we stayed at the mission
so the children could at least go to school
rarely out of work was he
on the properties all around
then down to Mildura for the fruit in season
Grace smiling as she told me about her man

I saw you in uniform you know
speaking softer and slapping my knee
in Broken Hill
you heading off to war
it should have been called broken heart not Broken Hill
so sure I was you would be killed
couldn't even bring myself to step forward from the crowd

then said I honestly
emphatically
I wish you had
our lives would not have been the same
I'd given you up by then
well and truly convinced you'd be wed
but in a heartbeat I'd have grasped your hand

to which Grace thought for a moment
then without a tear but with a soft smile replied
yes and that may well have been so
but everything is meant to be
I wouldn't trade my family for anything and nor would you Jack
we all have our what might have beens
but childhood friends we shall always be

hard times but so glad we had them eh
said Grace as we did finally say good night
but knowing that we would see each other soon again
she recently moved to Dubbo to be with family
we now visit each other almost weekly
just friends mind
we've both had our partners our children and our passions

yet nothing nothing now quite warms my heart
like when my old friend comes to visit
we light a fire outside
I make the tea strong as she always liked it even as a child
we laugh at the two old fools we are
gazing up at the stars that are just as young as they were
on the track camped beside a water cart

an old upright piano I have
Ewan learning to play for a time as a boy
sure I was that Grace would enjoy it
but she never did learn how to play
such a pity said I *you had such hands for it or a violin*
but as she does her words breathe of reality
and nice it would have been too if there'd been money and a hope for lessons

we speak often of course of those old times
not entirely but it is always there
somewhere in the hours of meeting
some memory we want to either check or share
and not long of course before the topic was raised
of two rough stones
and where they both were

the first time she visited out my way
Grace came with her daughter Violet too
I'd put together a lunch as best I could
and then next to the pot of tea
I placed a small calico knot that had been many years with me
I wonder Violet too
if this little thing would stir any memories in your mother

her daughter did not immediately to me seem
the daughter of Grace in every way
a much larger woman physically
a calm person within her middle age
very quiet at first appeared
but deeply intelligent like her mother
and quickly enjoyed this puzzle and Grace's reaction

oh Jack
you still have that there
here was me just the other night
wondering but afraid to ask
and she sat with eyes fairly sparkling
leaning across my kitchen table
helping her daughter ease the cloth from its firm knot

once undone the face of Violet seemed doubly puzzled
perhaps expecting more of a treasure than a humble rough stone
but her mother beamed even more at the sight
giving off a small gasp and a squeal
and immediately relishing the retelling of a special tale
now my girl
now this is a thing you hold there in your hands

this stone my dear
I passed to Aunty Hannah Quayle
so many many years ago
there is another to make the pair
that I hold dear
have kept safe for sixty something years
but I can't believe that you Jack did the same

never was it in doubt I confirmed
even at war
it was as safe as I could make it
at the base of my old kit bag
Grace just held it for a while
rolled it from palm to palm
well now then Jack isn't this little stone something to see

I just a girl and Jack a boy
and some time after we'd had to go our separate ways
Jack's father sadly taken from us
and me with Mum down Weinteriga by then
then one day my father arrives
at least the man who for a time was with my mother
he comes after many months gone away with these two stones and a story

Hector was his name
and not a bad man when all was said and done
a battler that was true
and like many quite fond of the drink
but for a time helped my old mother along
and took me with him on his water cart
where Jack and his dad so well I got to know

and that was the thing Jack
looking back
I think he so admired your dad
a solid man so he was your dad
sober is what stuck with me
calm and confident you could say
like a true compass in a place and time when many did lose their way

so Hector then arrives this day at Weinteriga
by that time he on a bicycle
like many in those days
up and down the river
limping from one shearing shed to the next station
amazed my mother often later said she was
that this time he arrived sober and giving over such treasures

to me Jack it was the example of your dad
that made Hector do such a decent thing
and never did we see him again
after that most interesting day or so
that old cart remained who knows where and your horse too
and off he journeyed on his endless track
feeling perhaps that we were safe there and he'd done a decent thing

anyhow the yarn he carried
was that he'd been way up river
when he heard from another and then another
of Old Tom's bullocks found wandering
out Wanaaring way in the shade of the whim of a bore
felt some kind of need said he
on account of Jack's father to therefore venture for himself to see

said he saw not a single bullock
not surprising by then they had been purloined into new homes
yet after a week or so of tracking
came across the rotten corpse
water there was still in a flask by its side
death to a cause unknown
he buried him there though there was no weeping upon the grave

Hector reckons then he went straight to Bourke
reported the death and the place of the find
saying that the only thing he did not tell that constable
was the matter of them two stones found in his clothes
knowing them not to be the dead man's after all
he saw no wrong in the taking of them
thinking more likely Jack's dad was the source of any gem

now of course I've no proof
of any I am about to say
and it upset my mother no end
when I found the courage to share this with her
she would have nothing of it
but Jack I'd be keen to know your ideas
perhaps it was Hector the cause of Old Tom's demise

now at this did Violet come even more alive
her eyes wide fixed on her mother
then gazing at me
hoping for an answer or confirmation
there were many yarns out that way then
I offered briefly
Old Tom had many enemies with Hector definitely being one

Violet and I both looked to Grace
eager to know what her theory would be
I'm not sure of course it was he
imperfect though he was
I'm not convinced he had murder within him
but perhaps it was revenge for your father Jack
a man he did truly admire

one thing that did never add up to me
was how Hector would ever have found
a single corpse out among that vast country
if as was said already separate was he
from his precious bullocks and any trail
perhaps it was a man alive and walking Hector followed after all
and maybe make more sense why we saw nothing of that man again

what Grace suggested did make sense no doubt
and with both women looking to me
and with so many years intervening
between whatever deed done and that conversation in my kitchen
I thought why should we not then decide it
allow the only people with any connection or care
to determine clearly something at last

well then Grace
let us just leave it at that
he may certainly have done as you suggest
such was his feelings perhaps for my dad
and if he and your Afghan father both
had been slain by that Old Tom
well Hector may have welcomed such a just opportunity

as close to the truth as ever we may get
so why not give us at least some peace of mind
agreed then
and one thing Hector certainly did do
was be forthcoming with these two stones
shall I tell you then both
what was said to me of they

Violet handed my stone across to me
she and Grace had until then shared it between them both
as if confirming it was my turn to speak
before anything else Grace
it occurred to me to ask
do you know anything of Jack and Hannah Quayle
I saw nothing of them all these subsequent years

Grace gave a soft smile and a shake of the head
Aunty Hannah yes but only once or twice
and not since Uncle Jack died
even that back in thirty something before the war
older but just the same she was
such knowledge and such energy
to pass so much language and all else onto her young ones

Uncle Jack too though
think of him just as you knew him
his own man to the last
you'd hear not a bad word of them both
by whitefellas or from any other
and I left Grace a moment to her thoughts
before mother and daughter again both looked to me

Hannah and Jack Quayle
arriving at Kallara when they did
presented me so unexpectedly
with this little treasure here
and once explained by Hannah that the other half was with you Grace
the point was clearly made
that two should one day be reunited and returned to their proper earth

you do still hold it do you Grace
for if so why should we not
out of respect do just that as requested
Grace herself was nodding in immediate agreement
while Violet looked upon in a wonder
perhaps she had not imagined this visit to her mother's ageing friend
would ever hint at mystery and intrigue

ye do have it don't ye mum
surely ye do she almost squealed at the idea
of course child of course now I do
always safe with me it has been
to which Violet well alive now decided
that's it then
it's me who'll be driving to White Cliffs when you choose

*

we chose to wait for some slightly cooler months
with Grace determined though to be back at home
before this referendum at the end of May
hopeful that with it would come much celebration
a yes vote long overdue she explained
meaning Aborigines would actually be counted in any census
and the government have the power to make laws for them

we have a way yet to come
she said finally as we made our plans
this place still might yet be
a decent country and perhaps even offer harmony
and I so do hope that is the way the vote falls
each step after all is not without flaw
but as with our Federation even imperfect steps are a way forward

the plan then we devised
not for a nation but small steps at least for us two friends
if for reasons known only to a few
was to travel to the grave of my father
and at his feet
buried shallow
would soon be two rough stones returned

returned to a decent man
who it may be presumed
had been entrusted them by some struggling Chinese
they were perhaps a gift from them
for much assistance already given
much would never be know
but it seemed the right place for them to be

then in another important way
will this be a fine thing indeed
these stones of the rainbow returned
where Uncle Jack's creator first touched the earth
so much has been wrought from the ground
right across this amazing land
returning two humble stones is the only thing for Grace and I to do

www.ingramcontent.com/pod-product-compliance
Lightning Source LLC
Chambersburg PA
CBHW070922080526
44589CB00013B/1399